HIGH SACRIFIC

JOHN F. DEANE

High Sacrifice

THE DOLMEN PRESS

HIGH SACRIFICE is designed by Liam Miller, typeset in IBM
Journal Roman and printed in the Republic of Ireland by
Patternprint Limited for the publishers, The Dolmen Press,
Mountrath, Portlaoise, Ireland.

Publication of this book was assisted by a grant from An
Comhairle Ealaion (The Arts Council).

First Published 1981

British Library Cataloguing in Publication Data
Deane, John F.
    High Sacrifice
    I. Title
    821'.914 PR6054.E/Pbk/

      ISBN 0 85105 383 1 *Special Edition*
      ISBN 0 85105 383 3 *Pbk*

CONTENTS   Page

ACKNOWLEDGEMENTS

I acknowledge the help given by Barbara, my wife, by
Dick Roche, David Marcus, Emmanuel Kehoe, Ciaran
Carthy, Jack Harte, Aine McEvoy and John Quinn.

Irish Press New Irish Writing; Irish Times; Ulster Tatler
Literary Miscellany; Cyphers; Omens, Leicester; Poetry
Review, London; Cracked Lookingglass, London;
Writing in the West, Connacht Tribune; Cork Examiner;
The Tablet, London; Dublin Opinion; Honest Ulsterman;
U.C.D.Broadsheet; Stony Thursday Book; Reality;
Studies; R.T.E. Radio One.

FOR MY MOTHER AND FATHER
GRATEFULLY

ISLAND

It is June; sun lolls along the Achill bog;
the hill seems softened and its jutting fort looks
a delicate thing; the road curves sweetly here
by bog deal spines dug up for carving to adorn
new sideboards; robin and wren are busy
through fuchsia by a graveyard wall where golden
iris sucks up moisture from the soil; oh summer,
soft summer. Man greets man loudly along
rhododendron aisles, mothers whisper proudly
of daughters at communion rails, while across the bridge
the tourists' cars rush in, klaxoning at freedom.

In the ditch below the road a house squats, you
know what it's like inside: two brothers and two
sisters frozen into winter: there is a cold
dumbness and hot frothings in the brain; now old,
grown furtive, they can scream at times, strike out, fling
crockery and rush against the door. They live
of charities and scrape a crazy patch of ground.

Ah but the world keeps burning brightly; against a pane
outside, such blunder and are lost, betrayed by
some demand of entropy. Cars pass on the road,
a lace curtain stirs, a face peers out and smiles.

THAT MAN

Long summer evenings as the sun set
he would drive back to Keel for fishing; once,
when sea stroked shore as if peace had been declared,
he walked from the pier briskly,
along field's edge towards the headland; on his left
the ocean, on his right fields sloping to a far village.

Exhilaration in the lark's song
and half-heard background of the seagulls' calls -
softness of mossy ground and the up and down
of turfy slopes and hillocks;
the fishing-rod in his hand, there was a song
silent in his soul, giving spring to his long stride.

Here and there slugs were spreading themselves
before his feet, bodies of slime and mucous
stuff nauseous to the thought; these he avoided
left them to thrush and blackbird.
He passed the cove where things were festering down
in the cold dark where sea cut deep under the land.

At last, from the furthest point of rock
he began to fish, and soon I saw him catch
a pollock, heavy as stone, flabby as seaweed;
he would not put his fingers
into its gills to snap its back - I heard slap
of its body from a man's height, down on rocks; it left

traces of moist dirt among scales,
blood-stains. From that man's seed I came,
out of wastes like oceans, through blood I was born
into this world and began
to swim free of him; I too, fell subject
to the pain and the wonder of that long journey home.

WATER

The sea is a world of silence, like our
deep night with stars we imagine
motionless. Mackerel shoals move swiftly as our
dreams, following in their millions some weaving
miracle. I stand alone to-night on the quay;
there is no moon; at my back the world I know,
solid, irreversible; before me the ocean,
mind's obstacle, fluid world, unquestioning. Beneath
my feet there is the groan of wooden
beams, querulous sound of waters. I have to guess
those myriad half-world things where tide meets land.

The trawler drifed far this morning, our world
shrinking to a tossed mote against immensity
and yet our nets were full, mackerel slapped out
rhythms of death on our pitched planks, their
rainbow artistry dimming at our touch;
o yes, our lives are water but our heat
is blood. To-night I cannot say where sea
ends and sky begins; there is a sudden web
of rain; I wish you peace, sea-world, as I face
towards the light, wondering if our tamed night
has strung its mesh somewhere across our flux.

COVE

God knows how many millions of years the sea
has sucked and slopped, has reared raced reached and thudded
against the high walls of the cove, where sunlight

never penetrates beyond a few feet down
the black-hewn sides; the carcass of a cow lies
wedged in the rocks and seaweed, the sleek sheen of its

putrefaction heaving on the tides.
Out in the bay a curragh stalls; two men fish
for mackerel, a third skillfully oars the old

boat still; long lines of feathers, slowly turning
hooks, trail deep below the belly; hands, rough as
dry shore rocks, touch the cord lightly; when a shoal

strikes, there is excitement, almost sexual
as messages of life and struggle, blood and scales,
of ocean mysteries, pulse out of long-dead

centuries into a waiting, black hewn brain.

ISLAND WOMAN

It wasn't just the building of a bridge,
for even before, they had gone by sea
to Westport and from there abroad, and each
child sent money home till death in the family
brought him, reluctant, back. Of course the island
grew rich and hard, looked, they say, like Cleveland.

On a bridge the traffic moves both ways.
My own sons went and came, their sons, and theirs;
each time, in the empty dawn, I used to pray
and I still do, for mothers. I was there
when the last great eagle fell in a ditch.
My breasts are warts. I never crossed the bridge.

NEXUS

Slievemore megalithic tombs and deserted village

There is a silence in the golden eagle's
absence, when only wheatears scold from barren
folds, winds move or, high along the mountain, sheep
plead; - bird to bird, slope to slope, wool carded
by the storms. Tied down by bracken, megalithic slab
tombs nothing, pyre flamed out four thousand years
ago; black-sleeked hearse now shambles by, its sad
islanders rosaried along a track to gather
by the white stone graves; - bone to bone, rock
to rock, ash spiralling on the winds. I stand
where famine raped an entire village; beyond
lie cliffs and sea, primeval shuffling of bog,
mid-morning along the houses, sounds from a school
and node calling to node out of the spun world.

WOMAN

Down by the river wild iris grows, fuchsia
makes a graveyard wall. She had begun to yearn
for it, secretly, as for the myriad-coloured
quilt, homely and warm at the end of her
scrubbed day. Hands rubbing idly in her apron
she stood at her door, gazing; generations
she had watched ease into that gallery
of rosaries and flower-bowls and now her deepest
prayer was vague, from some darkness in her
to a child in her when, sometimes, she visited
after her bulked sons had eaten. She knew
the individual signatures of shells and
coloured glass in that haphazard acre. When
they chained the graveyard gate, opened another
plot naked to the winds, bleak, where kestrels fly, her
spirit guttered and went out. Hers is the first
grave, by a grey wall and traffic hustles by.

BUNNACURRY PIER

where we sifted sands for lug-worm when the tide
had dropped away (as peace does) baring rocks,
mudflats soft (as pain is) here where we shied
stones to scud across the water, plop into dusk;

our laughter scampered over eggs of terns
(as if, love, pain were not yet born) evenings
like this, misted to brown and grey, the pier
slopped in its seaweed, its crabs and sprats moving

though we could shrug off darkness for we called
only each moment life: (I need to share
my island with you, love, and with our child
let this pier head off currents for a time) there
friends lived, this house now boarded, darkness walled
by dampness, windows without panes (love, look aside)

GILLIN NA LEANBH

Wife, child and I turned east from Dugort
strand, passed up by promontary forts
of the iron age, stood where sea-thrift
has worn the spiralling centuries, on a cliff

over the Atlantic; a patch of turf
lies sunk between field and cove on the damp edge
of nowhere. We stumbled on neglected, rough
slabs uninscribed and hidden now by sedge,

that mark where unbaptised were locked
in unblessed cells; misshapen, wailing things
half-born, hustled lives whom neither God
nor devil coveted, buried here when rings

of mist were beading round the moon; cachette
for pain, limbo, on the borders of being,
will any resurrection ever knit
life's proud continuum these children broke?

LIOS CEARRA

It is a communal celebration, this,
3 men from one village.

              An engine clangs to life
startling gulls from seaweed coils; the harbour smells
of shark oil; dogfish float, their decomposing
bodies nose the pier.

              Oilskins, boots, are cumbersome
on the small half-decker. One, as is his custom,
invokes the saints, the Baptist, Peter, Patrick,
John. Outside the harbour mouth an iron cross
has stood through centuries, its base in concrete
on the sea bed.

              The trawler moves jauntily now
in the spirit of winds and tide; island edge,
sea-smells, dead war-mines like beehive huts in grass,
the spirits of evil exorcised - water's
exhilarating kingdom, rigging iike bells
along the dark; cliffs far off are pillars, a statue
in its niche withdrawn into the shadows. Here,
it is new life, nets fill.

              When wreckage touches
shore, others will find the bodies, souls have bccn
claimed for Christ, by water. It is a communal
celebration, this, people lighting candles
in the bright day, slowed to sorrow
by the mystery of the sacrament they
share in when the bell calls.

                    Bodies anointed
in oils, three more names written down
among their island people, Sean, Patrick, John,
now clothed once more in their white garments.

Achill Island, July 1979

BOATYARD

The town grew up around it, sang and loved; now
it is a blotch along seascapes. Rust has crept
over the high cranes, a tilted tractor's windscreen
is cobweb-cracked and a crazy acreage of junk
sprawls hopelessly. Tree-trunks have been ravished here,
abandoned to beach-combing winds; odd fires burn,
piled planks are scorched-out wigwams and I know
grey rats hold jamboree under the moon.

Ships that are ghosts ride out from church-high galvanized
sheds, process through cheers down slipways into times
when storms hauled heroes high into whipping dark
and waves spread out for wonder their still, green depths.
In mud beyond, a naked two-funnelled wreck
was a missionary's hymn on coasts of Africa.

In one tight corner they are moulding cabin
cruisers for the rich, of fibre-glass and plastics;
here is a world that cries for kings or prophets
or for some brazen whore to spirit pride back
along these coasts; the traders have grown fat, moved
back, a little higher up the hill, digging
the earth, laying new pipes, lighting new fires.

SEA-SMELL

On mud, here in our backwater, when tide
seeped away a while, I found a blue shark
beached in death's abject flabbiness; that such
stern royalty should sicken in shallow
estuaries, along tin-can shorelines, seemed

obscenity. Gulls had begun essential
scavenging towards life's fearful symmetry:
shit trickling down sleek belly: squirming things
of white busy in a curved slit of terror
that was its mouth - only the eye still masterful,

round largeness of it riveting as if
remembering fierceness out of sudden dark,
knife beauty of its form along incredibly
voracious depths. Sea-smell of rot already
wafting round our bay, witness to wild grief

of being, need to grasp this universe, swallow
as if it were fleshed sex of woman wholly
down within but see! we blush and nod, stalk
concrete streets of our estates, hating grass
in cracks, glad to turn a key in the small front door.

THE FORT

I will reach the stack on a low tide;
scrambling over seaweed, shingles, pools,
I will climb rough secret steps of stone
spiralling to cathedral silence;
sea-thrift, miracles of multicoloured flowers
hide in crevices, webbed among the folds
of the old cliff's face. On top, a fort was built
so long ago the stones have soldered

to the rock. Here I can sit and laugh
to think how we strain to build
fortresses of our days, raise bulwarks
against the tides, intricate security
systems against theft. Here I can join

my mind to the stone's smoothness,
language to the squawk of kittiwake,
dreams to dust-packed ledges. Tide
comes in around me, will pause,
then ebb again. Soon I will wander
back to my desk in the fools' fortress.

THE WOOD

I stood in a grove of pine trees, rain
swathing the world in grey. Long-dead pine
needles covered vaults of putrefaction,
there was a dimness of aisles, a dome
channelling waters; toadstools stood proud

between humped tree-roots and the wet boles
looked black marble pillars. All things were
interpenetrating, as of particles;
thought, memory were lulled away, till I
seemed somewhere out of body shaping

and reshaping, like a still alder
under the weight of day. Outside, rain
eased, but branches kept rhythmically
channelling drops as imperceptibly
from everywhere, perfume grew, delicate

as a phrase from long-forgotten prayer
ghosting through memory: I stood alone
non-initiate among some congregation.
It was then the ferret came, busy
among cones, sharp eyes and body tensed

to life; he saw me rigid as if surprised
in crime, stared for some moments, seeming
to accept and busying towards me.
A voice startled from the road, calling,
and at once ferret, incense, silence

vanished into a dull and unblessed day.

23

QUESTIONS

He walks the roads of Achill, always with the same
old cap; we meet, he raises that cap to shout
confident assertions about earth or sky, then laughs

out of his belly. He has no tests to put
to life or God, but waits outside till sermon's done
to eye parades of jeans or blouse into his

church, then kneels on cap inside the door, great
red hand urging his chin to prayers. Between
wet dawn, dung-yard at dusk, death harries him

but he survives, whistling, though his eyes can sharpen
as peregrine's after prey, for he too, lives where cliffs
ride out naked, and mists visibly corrode; I

have questions I would like to ask him, but not now, not now.

ACOLYTE

We set out to build a compelling edifice,
to cluster pillars over naves, arches that climb
to vaults dark with a hoped-for presence,
exuberant facades, buttresses and capitals
awesome in sculpted detail, spires that rest
higher than mere eagles - writing our hymn
to the perfectability of man. Winds come,
storms suck out the sky; cities shape
and split around our walls; we wait for the days
to make our lives' historiated columns
a sounding organ to the glory of our God.

Our island chapel was simplicity,
rectangles, verticals and plain glazed windows.
When the world hung right, glory came
multicoloured through our one rose-window. I learned
to serve at stations of the cross, around our walls
figures in relief enacted that far-off story;
heavily we sang, stabat mater dolorosa. At times
the eye would follow a purple flower, opening
in light on the wall, its petals moving higher.

Each Spring, reluctantly, my father went to spade
scraws from our bog into a drain, unbandaging
old sores, probing again for the earth's fires.
Slean sliced through flesh, pitching soft shapes high
onto the bank; we spread them out, wet hands cold,
fingertips leaving tracks like claws of a scared
animal; the man dug down, leaving neat spits,
water rose as he sank, dark blood around the scalpel.·

At times I fashioned sods, like putty, to shape
of house or man, but the wind dried them in hours, twisted
age through them, wrinkled them shapeless. Then, like a god,
I joyed to break them, hear the stretch and snap
of a million fibres. Within weeks the bank,
as a man when the fire has left him, lay
in patterns of earth, a veined trickling of water.

Our two-roomed school steamed with learning;
on bent backs a rhododendron wand beat rhythm
to our sing-song lore. Brothers of St Francis wore
soft brown habits and white knotted cincture;
in their monastery chapel terracotta statues
smiled down on polished floors. We learned of God,
of Abraham and Noah, of towns outside
our island, colours beyond our skies. Once,
on the rhododendron driveway after a night
errand to the monastery, a barn owl hooted, each
gap in bushes sprang cowled figures without face.

We built the turves in dolmens
under a March sky, glimpsing
white of a young girl's thighs
in the sharp winds; the bank
was hardening now, the thin
scab of drying peat had formed
for another year; tiny
skeleton chapels spread out
along the field. It was all
drudgery, back ached, hands froze,
young minds clogged and sagged those days.

Changes in the rubrics of those days
were cataclysmic; the day grandfather died
a car called for us at school; aunts came
from Waterford to offer sympathy but
made our play anathema. That slow
walk to the graveyard was mesmeric, voices
intoning rosaries, mystery
fastened under brass on polished pine. God was
omnipresent to those days, creator,
sovereign Lord of Heav'n and Earth and of All
things; grandmother's tears were linked to those
of a delicate Christ on the mantlepiece;
neighbours took charge of the tea or packed
the fire in against the night. And soon
it was school again, bible history, and games.

There was a grove of pine trees by our house;
ground there was carpeted in pine-needles
centuries deep; roots, unkempt and naked, bulged
over soil. High on a knot of branches I built
my house of wood, nailed it to the bark;
drops of resin hardened into pearls. I sat for hours
inside the turbulence of storms, branches creaked,
the green pine-needles brushed and whispered.
Beyond, the rain fell sidelong and out on the road
the adults sped, remote and monstrous dwellers
among stone; I was delegate to the conference
of elements until at dusk the rook armadas
came noisily around me; I was called
in to recite the rosary and climbed,
reluctantly, down, hugging the knuckles of my tree.

Rosary round a fire, words patterning made ethers
where we circled; clock ticked loudly, embers stirred.
Into such murmurings there came the miracle
of cockroaches from their prehistoric caves, my eyes
followed their ritual dance while the words sounded:
"sinners, now and at the hour of our death."
One night my grandmother, big-bodied love, like God,
pincered one in tongs and dropped it on the fire - quick
sizzle, spit of flame. Through rosary I heard
screams of a total pain, helplessness become
somewhere all purgatory, all hell, but still
55 black beads went circling, telling mysteries.

We stumbled through our groves of Latin, the priest
chanting to a tabernacle; we were followers,
drawn along with cruet, censer, bell. Behind us
the men claimed territory, resting a knee
on a cap or Sunday hanky, staking out
their piece of floor against God's coming. We served
High Mass; around us priests moved in imponderable
black; a coffin lay on its chariot, with its guard
of high brown candles, and a slow chant dark
with omen filled our world: "Dies irae dies illa"
day of wrath, that dreadful day. Charcoal burned,
incense rose to a distant God who asked
for sacrifice before his altar-steps.

There are no monastic glories on our island,
no tales of miracles; on this unsheltered,
not quite barren soil, no saint made hermitage;
God happened in, settled down to stay. In one
valley by Slievemore's knees, a Mission to change
the island's ways from popery, grew; soup

was welcomed, oaths were said, the little church
so newly built was almost filled; but this was just
a bog fire, burning of heather till the crops
flowered and the soup cooled. The settlers
huddled tight into the mountain's lap.

> *"Slievemore Slievemore you are standing there*
> *With your head so high and your sides so bare;*
> *Some day some day you will surely fall*
> *And bury the colony jumpers all"*

Sod piles on sod and the clamp grows; one takes charge,
finally, to build and edge, to shape a sloped
oratory against a gable wall or by a road's
edge. This is the circle's end, individual
sods gone hard and dry for burning; there is a pride
in work completed. Someone brings a rush
basket, breaks open a wall, makes a hole
in the hard flank; now is the start of decay,
the shapely edifice disfigures, and each
mid-morning, someone comes out a back door
scattering ash from a bucket over the land.

CANTICLE OF THE CREATURES

Most high, omnipotent good Lord, yours
is glory and all honour; no man is worthy
to breathe your name; you light the day for us
by your great power and the night is proud for you
in stars and moon - *o see the river swelling*

at my feet - yours the winds and the wild sky
and the air that nourishes your creatures; yours
the fresh, pure water - *now but a fragment*
of city wall restrains the tides where I tramp
forgotten layers of brain and bone - the fire

in its mastery speaks forth your praise,
the earth, o Lord, sustains us all, and waits;
the roses in their beauty whisper you, *they reach*
out thorns and prick against my flesh, yet praise
to you who can forgive, remembering our walls

the little foxes have broken through, whose sheer
perfection sings your name; yours the glory
in our death, shame, sin are ours and the pain
in the deep sting; *somewhere the cherry is blossoming*
again; most high creator, yours the glory.

31

LOURDES

We came out of a world of clouds massed
in purity, and where blue glows delicate to deep;
sun on a boeing's wings, bolts, steel shimmering
to wafer white, beautiful as a kittiwake high
against immensity; we were sitting, pressurized,
with our seatbelts fastened, dreaming.

                                          Woman,
at your grotto my fingers touched wet rock, cave
gaping, black; world of candles perpetually
burning, of shuffling silences where only sparrows
chatter, where we joined a mass of crumpled minds,
of bodies gnarled and knotted into pain and strapped
down onto their stretchers. *Que soy era Immaculada
Councepcion.* Above our drones of aves, beyond
grey clouds, a jet was flying on, following the sun.

LOVE POEM

It was a weary night, as of ashes
    brooding; in the wood we lay
under a lovely star. I had a sense
    of ending, of a year passing away
among trees, as of machines
    throbbed to silence. We made
love on the earth's floor, our beings
    pulsed under the strain
of a stored energy; somewhere there was
    soft cry of pain as two bodies flamed
into one fire. It was over; that night
    you had conceived our child.

ESTATE

Waste ground outside our walls is heron-wild, weed-lush
by stagnant ponds; the elms are dead, high skeletons
that brandish rooks and jackdaws in their bones;
sometimes, near dusk, the mallard move, fly low, and whir
back home from somewhere, as does sorrow;
at night, when the city stills,
there is rustling of rats, and sounds
as of vegetation seeping into rot; the frogs spawn
and the spirit of an old, old god moves across the waters.

We cultivate our garden day by day, set out for work
or hang blanched sheets high up along the winds;
ah then my love, when our lives sag, quivering under the long
questioning of days, I can only hold your slight
sad shape against me, and make you gasp
into awareness of my need.

FROM CLIFFS AT HOWTH

Our lives manipulated order now,
rain-water channelled along concrete runnels
to the taps. We will resent the serious tramp,
the tricks winds play around the house, we miss
the jocularity of a rock's ridged face
under the sun.
        Small gardens offer
appointed order of hyacinth bulbs,
of autumn fires.
        I am waste ground
between estates, island water, wrens
around spring-wells; I am
plush draylon suite and tinted sherry glass. Here
at day's sinking, I can image
shearwater's flight where seas in turmoil
expose creation's bedrock to the clouds.

JOHN STOKES ESQ.

He never laboured the bog before his house
into a garden nor the bog behind his house, into wheat fields;
with others he scuffed in our dole queues, wandering over years
- bog-asphodel along the moors - dreaming of gold
in high sierras, sun's rays awesome on great brazen wheels;
his house was thrown onto the earth, like a leather patch on worn
trousers; it was smoke and hobs, tales of old rickety gods.

Against our walls he battered prophecy, of Manannan Mac Lir, Lord
of the incredible deep, whose home is whisperful under long mists
and forked caverns of the mountain-top: *"in the last times
only a patch on Slievemore's crown will be held dry
out of the world-engulfing floods."* He died, and his house stands
boarded eave-high in the sun's bounty.

Sometimes I see, among loomings and windings of streets,
clerks through office windows become heroes tall as gods
in torques of gold, the silent proper people rising in the lift
go soaring to a mountain summit, and then I smile
the unacceptabe smile of the mad John Stokes.

MOMENT

Countless fetid scurryings precede this moment,
moment that is pitiful, like offal. You
come screaming down a night road, under lights;
between your thighs a throb of power, your hair
ghostly about your face in a false breeze, you
ride, arms widespread on handlebars, a dervish
under trance. World spins, night is deep but ashen.
It seems to be the curve that beats you, you explode
out of life's sepulchral chamber, off kerb to paling,
motorbike bursting to a somersaulting shower
of tin and glass, engine's pride gouged into silence,
headlamp, like your spotlight, dims to black, you are
flicked off the apex of this pyramid oh
all directions into eternity. By dawn, tiny things
absorb the red-black blood that has seeped out of your head.

FROM A BUS SHELTER

There are bones rattling out there, there is flesh
raw and live being fanged in an un-
mentionable anguish, there are terror-frozen
children savaged by packs of wolves and in
swamps men writhe with bellies burst from
frenzy of fierce boars; and if you face it you
can almost hear them, feel them, just out there
beyond fine films of rain darkening
the long street, under klaxoning of cars that
scuttle somewhere, camouflaged by humps
of black umbrellas bobbing by, between the misted
dimly-lit bus windows and the faces staring
out - but it is best to huddle in an overcoat and
listen to the streetboys shout the evening news.

EXCAVATIONS

They have built Christchurch on a hill.
From under its black arch you can see them now
excavate the hill, mark off excitedly baubles of glass,
flitches of bone, things dead, indifferent, long burnt out.
Like rivers they are fingering the mortar, may stir
the rocks of the cathedral; belfry, gargoyle, buttress
down about their brains.
          You can see me walk
that hill, stagger a little, though morning; what you see
you may not like: near-black, cobbled face, hanging
weather-beaten clothes. Somehow, I have forgotten
all my yesterdays.
          If I smile to you, and mutter, you
will pull away, back to your burden; I await
progress; my teeth have not gone brown for nothing, my smell
is of years of effort; I have expended all my energies
and burned holes into my eyes; I move towards
some synthesis, I will go up in flames and leave
a charred patch on the hill.
          To-day I'm free,
not burrowing, just waiting and a little hungry. To-night
I'll huddle under the cathedral walls, if they
have not fenced it off, unsafe. You see
they have built Christchurch on a hill.

DISCOVERY AT WOOD QUAY

They laid him with his spear at his right hand
even in rock, even in death; he had survived
flow of day and ebb of night for almost twenty

raw years; like me, like you perhaps, he too
had snarled his questions to the truculent
fraying down of time, unanswered, till a wild

call, down by the river, without city walls
brought him to elation of unreasoned hate;
he died, gratefully. They gave him a cell in boulder

clay, where he lay, waiting oblivion.
Then as the centuries trampled dust down
on his hiding-place he was glad for more time

as worms and obscene gnawings things had ceased their fret
and left too much of him: till you and I came knocking,
discovered him, scraped his bones back into light,

pathetic skull, thin bones; now you will take him out,
display him in your National Museum, poor
ragged hero for your cause - there

till the darkest secrets of the earth herself
fall before the frantic excavations that you do
into your own brain, your own soul. Oh you who pass

this transfixed nakedness, pity him, and blush.

MIRACLE IN THOMAS PLACE

Midnight light was freezing the back garden of number 9;
a man came out to piss before going to bed;
clouds tinted orange from the city lamps
passed, like lazy smoke-puffs, between man and moon;
the man pissed over a rose-bush,
put his hands in his pockets and hitched up his trousers;
stars were hanging about, some here some there;
he cleared his throat and spat into the rose-bush;
in the house beyond a bathroom light flicked off;
o the old, old earth, scaffolded on millions of years;
the pissing and the spitting will pay dividends, come spring D.
you can't be too careful these days, he said,
locking the door before going up to bed.

INTERLUDE

City nomad, 12-year-hard
in scutting, like a mouse
scurrying in his underworld,
survivor among bus-wheels
like dusty feral pigeons, him
I saw push his own
delivery truck up the long street,
chassis of a pram, buckled
under coal, holding his lane
among rush-hour cars;

down the other side, an old
bedouin of this city
pushing his time-flaked
hand-cart, empty, home; shuffler
out of urine-smelling pubs and
lord of the back-lane realm
still living, silent, somewhere;
stunted in shape and speech, hawk
in his own territory, he too
ignored all claims of cars;

between child and man, words
coughed across the street - an esoteric
song over the dunes - a laugh, then
they were gone. Lights changed
and I moved on, drove
out beyond their limits
into my own oasis where I too
survive; in the evening sky
clouds formed, and broke,
like a mirage.

HIGH SACRIFICE

After the agony of 1798 the inevitable surge
of Ireland onto freedom demanded a new
victim to sacrifice to its great myth; history
moves from point to point, and growth
requires an access of effort and therefore of
force; the energy required for a new synthesis
does not necessarily come from without, but
from an expenditure of what is growing
within; but nothing is constructed except at
the price of an equivalent destruction;
something must set the flame to the pyre; and
1798 demanded a high sacrifice of a young
man five years later to give the blood and pain
some meaning.

Robert Emmet: born 1778, executed 1803.

In Stephen's Green they are tearing buildings down,
bulldozers shuffle busily, gaps appear as if
suddenly, and you realise you can't remember
what was there. Always the buses, lorries, cars
go bundling by while Robert Emmet's statue
catches dust. Under his nose the taxis file,
and stop, and wait, then move away. His eyes
are focussed on a cinema a few steps
from the house where he was born; his hands are held
in a gesture of disbelief although his head is high.

Perhaps at night, if he can find a lull,
he will slip down and dodge across the street
into his house (antique shop now); from his own window
look back on Stephen's Green and watch
as on a television screen, the years replay. Heaven
may have a hall like that, where we will sit and see
the earth's crust form and grow, the ape begin to stand
erect and find his words - a fascinating game but
Emmet knows no one can edit now. There were nights
he watched young girls waiting under gas lamps, when still

the Green was half a marshland and the city
died just down the street; dandelion puff-balls
floated on the air and Dublin's hoardes of beggars
sprawled in the ditch where gentry dumped their filth.
He has always walked the Green, when the beaux walked,
when captains strutted by with pretty cornet boys,
when souls crept from the Crusades, cowled in their
leprosy, seeking the lazar-house; all walked those stones
and all are gone. Sunpatterns now on the prams, sparrows
and leaves, where Emmet walks and he is wholly dumb.

I. MORNING

There has been a long heat;
dull, like silver, skies have sucked
dust out of the pavements; city
rocks like a mirage; from wheels
the haze presses, a balloon
swelling inside the brain. Night,
when it comes, is not night, not
black, sheets like jam against the thighs

not white; but there are dreams:
seas rising against a storm, moss
sponged along the back; dreams too
of the city bursting free in flames.

I dreamt last night of kneeling on a bank;
there was a king who swung an old mace, a packed
together ball of lead and spike; I accepted
with a faintly humourous wonder. My head
flew; bemused, I wandered among piled shells
I found the head, caving out and decomposed
with a grin tied on by strips of flesh; I could find
no pain. I noticed I had lost
my body though I knew it was a corse
conspicuous in priestly robes; I found it
soused in a shallow sea, putrid-grey and soft,
slobbering away when I tried to hold; now
I was outside time, could laugh, and go my way.

to Sarah Curran

In you I will be looking for
eyes that have not narrowed over death:
limbs that suggest
freedom beyond flesh, breasts that rise
gentle in pride.

I will bring a life needing to be
teased into quietness:
bones that are chill
by fear inherited.
Already

my name begins to rasp, to
roughen from erosion
of the past;
my blood is dark and needs
to be brought into the light.

I ask of you
high sacrifice, that I
may come when childhood themes
are severed
from my life.

I am longing for a child -
to see her stand in grass under the sun
and laugh a golden laugh like daisies -
to see her run along a hill
while her hair weaves songs out of the wind -

I long to watch with you
and tell young stories till she sleeps, and smiles;

I would fence her years with wonder
and lock answers out - let her tear
roses off a bush without a care, or prick -

I long to see her stoop, in silence, down
and kiss a weed, look up, and then forget -
her words her own, unhoned, as unrestrained
as furry creatures flitting in the trees;

I am longing for a child -
to lock her into liberty - and I
find my nights chained in fear.

47

I am not concerned with terror, it will pass,
I speak of fear. If I slip down old streets
into the past, beyond the darkness of uncultivated
realms, of course I hear things shuffling, whisperings
not human, and terror holds me; but beyond
there is a fear where utter dust
waits; shambling on its lanes old men have gone
straight into death; screams of childbirth hover
in its silence; what is not there has heaved
and spread its sperm of fear over the dust;
so if I claw at liberty, and hope
the clamouring men will swirl together
piking the towers of truth, I trust you
will understand; I am young and I intend
to cry down fear.

And what does it achieve? the dance.
Evening, onto a headland I saw them come
in slow procession, shackled to each other, all
shackled to a high plateau of stone. Perhaps
it was a dream I had, perhaps a question
that has always goaded; there, the centuries
crowded in a circle, deliberately flung
their shackles off the cliff and moved slowly
into the dance. Circling bodies found their own
rhythms, prayerful, like the rites of war - yielded
a golden nakedness where scars, blood burned
like myths, fires sprang out of their steps and stone
was an altar where the false gods burned - frenzy
to a rattle of bones, a triumph of pipes; at last
the initiates gathering burst to one vertical
flame, a sacrificial pyre, and vanished
in a breath of air. Perhaps it was a dream

I had. When the dance becomes a history
what has been achieved? for, shackled to each other
at dawn, onto a headland I saw them come.

INTERLUDE

MARSDEN:

I, too, ask to be pardoned;
when I have washed and vested, when I stand out
before you, high and mitred, I am not myself,
not he who sits alone at night, waiting to sleep,
and dreams. Of course we knew it all, word,
plan and gesture; we stepped always ahead of Mr. Emmet.
If he survived out of a long dying, then the same
hand from the altar cast its lot on him as it did me.
There is he who must become the emmissary goat
and he who must consign him to the devil
behind them both a gilded tabernacle
and relentless surge of struggle on to memory.
There is a voice calls Abraham when the swelling times
need wood and fire and holocaust;
there is a voice that spares, sometimes,
yet always there's a ram stuck fast
somewhere in other people's briars.
Do not judge harshly, then, my hand
over the victim; you have not seen my sleep or heard
the harsh breathing as I turn
restlessly on the march of night.

EVENING

I had hoped for time, with the tide
not yet on the turn - or as turf
piled strong, and night only
falling. There has never been enough
of time; already water
laughs about my throat, a cold
dawn hovers on the ashes.
I have watched sea-trout
burst in silver life over the waves near an old
patched-up net, and salmon fooled by light
onto a poacher's pike. There are eyes
watching, hands that betray, till the mind
is rushed and harried. I was that fool who strode
into an old circle, motley in green and gold,
my hat feathered as a jester's, my sword
without a blade. When the fire is lit, it is that
which licks up lives and spreads a fraud
called history. I will go down in embers
betrayed by the loud crackling of the days.

Up on the hills to-night the heathers burn;
from here there is but an orange gash in darkness;
I know that hare and skylark startle
into death, long-worked nests spit out
to nothingness, the ferns fizz into black;
it is the year's entropy and all is anger.
In a few days there will be silence, ashed
and crisp under the sun; a first fern, tentatively,
in a green that is almost white, will raise

one finger, clenched, moving;
when morning comes, I must face other things.

> I am to die
> to-morrow; I am aware
> of rooms where men
> settle to the hearth; I
> am alone, afraid;
> what I have been
> glimmers a moment on the wall,
> flicks out: my life
> a piece of paper flung
> on fire never taking
> flame; a black hole
> slowly from the centre
> writhed a while and
> swallowed in the rest;

When all is over, it is for myself
I die; under the indifference of pain
I will extract my individuality;
when body hangs on space, above the clutch
of crowds, I am alone to face my life;
my death is mine whoever comes to gape
or pray. There will not be one
place to claim me, for they will sever head
from body; my request that they will hide my flesh
from future generations, lest I lose
again what I have won in death;
if they wish, let them revere
a name, but let me rest in peace.

You say it was I who shouted and stood out
to take the lead? not so; if I but whispered
the room fell silent, made my words a boast,
if I laughed it was a threat, and if I loved
I was a patriot, my song a proclamation;

perhaps I never had a childhood, now
no matter. Across my nursery floor
stalked Tone and Napper Tandy: my bedtime tales
were parables of kingdoms; the virtues
of good government my father's grace at meals.

It may be dream or memory - from a branch
a corpse was hanging naked where winds crossed
and foxgloves grew. Like a fruit too ripe for
harvesters, it swung alone in its pendulum dance.
From that censer held to freedom, a stench
threaded along the breeze; a pitch-cap, like
a cock's comb, stood up on his head; his tongue
protruded as in mockery, his clenched fists
challenged mysteries. It was a clown's
stage; below his feet soldiers played at dice
laughed as though they had hung him there or could
cut him down and send him home. The sun
climbed into a clean blue sky but its beams
chilled me, chills like the clasp of a boned
hand, like the call in those empty, staring eyes.

My world has come
to a thin plank high
above the streets; wonder
if the noose was always

there, and the blindfold
darkening; the hangman
waits my signal that I
am ready; I have now
moments
of total freedom.

GARDEN

I came out of youth to a great house;
welcomed and bemused I stood with others
amid the ordered fragrance of geraniums
in the conservatory; in sandalled stillness
down corridors, I checked eyes inwards for He
was there; by a high altar, in fervour
of canticle and cope, I was clothed
in black. Gradually, memories of sea
and mountain ridge began to lie, and God's
words were echoing everywhere. The world turned
without me, seas were loud by cliffs and sea-
pink struggled against storms. *"Thou art beautiful,
beloved, a garden enclosed, a fountain sealed."*

MISSIONARY

Heavyweight wrestler for God, white beard
a waterfall down his soutane, he rose
like an old belfry above our novice years.

Stories he told us, colouring the edges
of our desert: witch-craft cowed by a lit
match, tribes by false teeth brandished; he

had crossed God's jungle carrying God's flag.
I wore a tightened cincture round my waist,
I lauded God round Kimmage grounds and heard

a voice from a blazing acacia bush call "Whom
shall I send?" Where a white-flecked blackbird sang
I knelt and cried "Lord here am I, send me, send me".

MATINS

We walked round shrubbery, cowled in silence,
somewhere in the long pause of mid-morning;
the fuchsia hung in scarlet, bees drew out
their honey; high trees benignly watched, long
used to circling figures on the gravel; we
read Rodriguez, his tome of huge wonders, deeds
of saints, glories of holiness, miracles
sprouting out of deserts. Secretly, I longed
that those naked whores spirited out of hell
into the monks' cells should tempt me, too;
I fasted, prayed, scaled the cliffs of sanctity
to no avail; always the sudden wren
distracted, a weed's unexpected beauty on a stone,
coolness of peas bursting against my palette; I
stayed in my tiny group, going round and round.

DISTRACTION

We were to praise aloud God's name at dawn
and plunge our sleep into enamel basins
of cold water, to move down corridors
shuffling off dreams, to choir, chant in unison
pattern of prayers, sink into meditation and dig
deep for God, each in his own soul.
I flogged my mule along Ignatius' path,
besieged Teresa's outer castle walls. One
beside me snored, Above the snickers, those
timid doves went scattering with a clatter of wings.
I thought of home, that trampling in aisles, that
rook-loud joy of Sunday suits, and in peace
I let my mind soar down over old fields,
exult in the roughness of the cold, wet cliffs.

LAUDS

"It is a question of praise" the novice
master said while his slender finger-tips shaped
a cage; "God will answer in the secret place
of thunder". In our cells we prayed, borrowing
words. Afternoons on the soccer field we
pitched against each other, savouring kick
on shin and shuddering shoulder charge, spat
curses into the free air. Later, in black
soutane and white surplice, God our judge,
ourselves the jury, we criticised each other
under seal of charity. Once, at night, sleepless,
I watched the moon grow white and fade through intense
silence, and I spoke obscenities to the bare
walls, out of the locked-in blackness of my soul.

AT A GRANDMOTHER'S GRAVE

That I should perform this office for you, seemed
profanity, you who had watched me from a child
assume the black and white of a minister
of the eternal mysteries; you had performed
such servile duties for me, now you lay
coffined at my feet.

            So I assumed a presence;
a childhood's incoherent love I distanced
from me, spoke in a grave, high tone: *De
profundis clamavi ad te Domine.*

Over my words hung a huge mid-morning
silence; beyond us the sluggish estuary, those
black-headed gulls about their squabbling; you
in that brown hole, I sprinkling water on you
from a plastic bottle.

            In my monastery cell
that night I watched pale light outline
my cassock hanging on the door, its folds
deep-shadowed, its shapelessness a figure lost
among great wilderness.

            Your face
is clay now; suburbs bulk around the cemetery
till view of the sea is lost; I stand, grateful,
with wife and child curb weeds from your small plot.

A BIRTH
for Catherine

Behind those portals the sacred rooms; something
of witchcraft, something of the contained silence
of cathedrals. Outside, the rough and
broken shoreline of city roofs that falls
off against the window.

An altar is prepared,
a naked body draped in the neophyte's
gown; this is a magic circle; there are
ministers.

All is timed in some inner impulse,
rhythms urgent as waves, power like that
splitting the earth's surface, pain
like flames in the devil's eyes as he rides
the dark; there are soothing rites and incantations,
a fierce breathing.

I hold your hand, helpless.
You sweat in this steel-cold, this bright
cleanness.

Now is a slipping off the brim
of the world, a clutching, screaming fall
till a cry, new and small, becomes for us our
exorcism, our ultimate benediction.